Where is Indy?

A Waverley Story Book for Children

Written by Amanda Stanford
Illustrated by Thomasson Burgess

The Reworkd Press
Charlotte, 2014

For wee Evie

WELCOM

Ding-Dong!

Indy! We are

here, come out

and play!

Where is Indy?

Is he behind

the door?

No?

Is he behind

the computer?

No?

Is he under

the table?

No?

Is he inside

the lampshade?

No?

Is he behind

the ball?

Yes!

We found him!

Goodbye, Indy!

About the author:

Dr. Amanda Stanford earned her PhD in English Creative Writing from the University of Edinburgh. She has taught writing and English classes for seven years in the US, Mexico, Japan, and Egypt. She also writes historical fiction under the pen name A M Montes de Oca.

About the illustrator:

Thomasson Burgess is currently a student at the University of North Carolina Charlotte, studying art education. She hopes to teach for a few years and then go into art therapy. This is her first book.